What Is A Rock

By B. John Syrocki, Ed. D.

Professor of Science

State University of New York

Brockport, New York

Pictures — Lucy and John Hawkinson

BENEFIC PRESS · CHICAGO

Publishing Division of Beckley-Cardy Company

Atlanta   Dallas   Long Beach   Portland

The WHAT IS IT Series

What Is A Bird

What Is A Season

What Is A Cow

What Is A Turtle

What Is A Fish

What Is A Chicken

What Is A Frog

What Is The Earth

What Is A Plant

What Is A Butterfly

What Is A Tree

What Is A Simple Machine

What Is Air

What Is A Magnet

What Is Light

What Is A Rocket

What Is Heat

What Is A Solar System

What Is A Cell

What Is A Machine

What Is Water

What Is Chemistry

What Is Sound

What Is Weather

What Is A Star

What Is Electricity

What Is A Bee

What Is An Atom

What Is Soil

What Is An Insect

What Is Gravity

What Is A Dinosaur

What Is A Rock

What Is Electronic Communication

CONTENTS

THIS IS A ROCK

A rock is solid, nonliving matter that is formed by nature. Rocks are found everywhere on top of the earth and under the earth.

A rock can be as big as a mountain

or as tiny as a grain of sand.

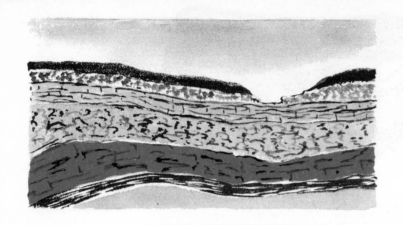

Rocks are found
near the top
of the earth,

deep in the ground,

and in the sea.

Some rocks are heavy.
Some rocks are light.
Pumice is a rock that
is so light it can float
on water.

Some rocks are smooth.

Others are very rough.

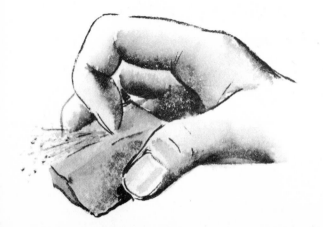

There are hard rocks
and soft rocks.
Some rocks come apart
when they are rubbed
with a fingernail.

Rocks are made of tiny crystals called minerals.

Crystals are like very small pieces of glass.

Different kinds of these crystals have different sizes, shapes, and colors.

Different kinds of rocks have different kinds of crystals.

Most rocks have two or
more kinds of crystals.
A magnifying glass helps
to show the crystals in
a rock.

Because of the crystals,
rocks show
beautiful colors.

HOW ROCKS ARE MADE

In deep places in the earth, there is a very hot, thick liquid. This hot liquid is melted rock matter. It is called magma.

Magma moves around under the ground. Magma moves up and sideways, too, if there are cracks in the earth for it to fill.

Slowly, most magma cools and hardens under the surface of the earth. It becomes rock.

Rock formed in this way is called igneous rock.

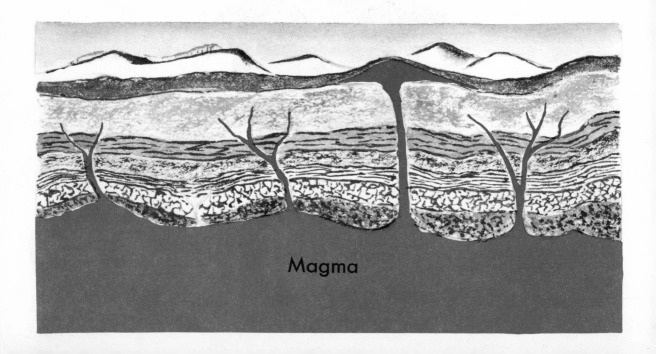

Magma

Granite

Feldspar crystals

Quartz crystals

Mica crystals

Large crystals form in these rocks that cool slowly.

Granite is one kind of igneous rock formed under the ground.

Granite has three kinds of crystals.

Sometimes magma does not cool in the earth. It may come up quickly and burst out of a volcano. Magma which reaches the surface of the earth and moves over the ground is called lava.

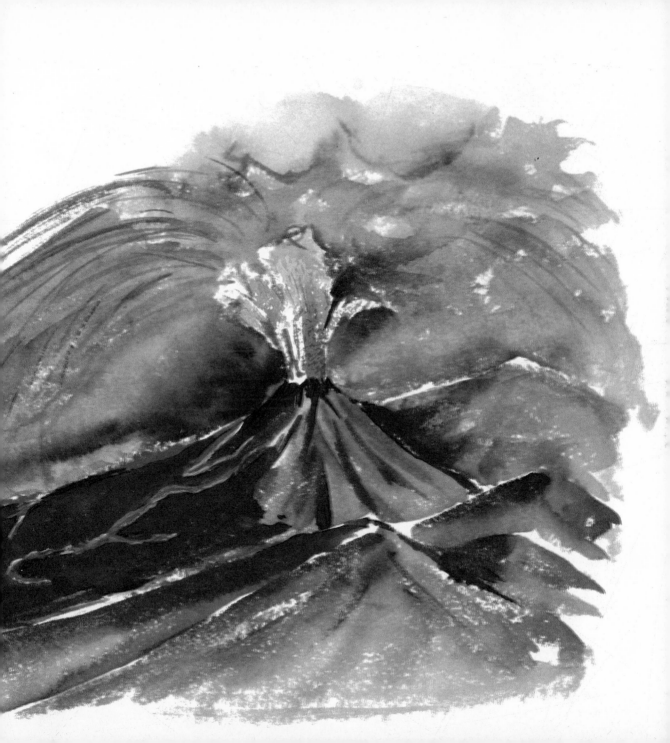

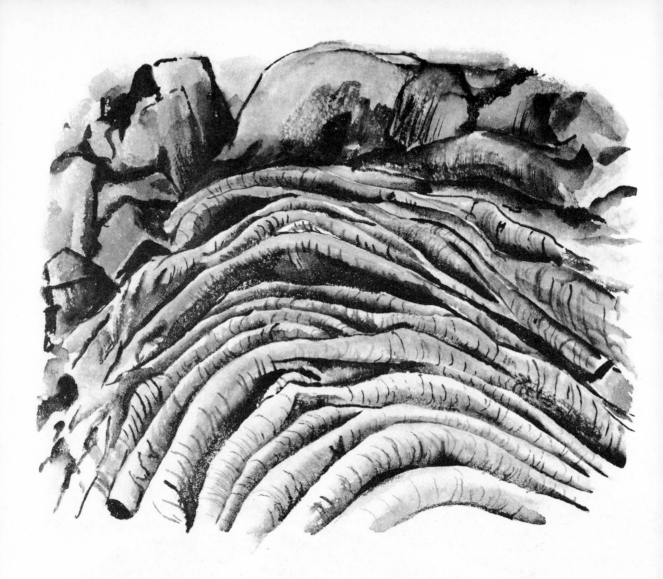

Lava cools very quickly and forms into rocks.
Sometimes it hardens as it flows.
Rocks formed from lava are also igneous rocks.

Rocks which cool quickly have very small crystals.

Some rocks are shiny.
They are like glass.

Black obsidian

Others are dull.

Volcanic breccia

Still others are full
of gas holes.

Pumice stone

Rock made of sediment, or sedimentary rock, is another kind of rock.

Sediment can be formed when rocks of all kinds are broken down into tiny pieces. These tiny pieces are carried from place to place by wind, water, or ice. The sediment is usually dropped in layers to form sedimentary rock.

One layer of sediment settles on top of another. After thousands of years, there may be many, many layers of sediment in one place.

Many layers of sedimentary rock can be seen in the Grand Canyon of Colorado and Arizona.

Sediment can be clear
sand. Grains of sand held
together by certain minerals
make a soft rock which is
called sandstone.

See how the tiny grains
are held together.

Sediment can be made
of sand and small pebbles.

A mineral can cement them
together to make a soft rock, also.

Not all parts of the
rock are the same size.

This rock is called a
conglomerate rock.

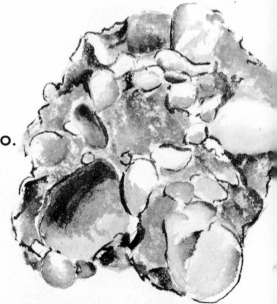

The shells of shellfish, falling to the bottom of the sea, also make sediments. Layers of shells, covered by mud and sand, pile up deep layers of sediments.

Other shells are not buried. They may cling together to form a rock like this.

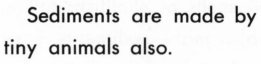

Sediments are made by tiny animals also.

Coral animals live in warm oceans. A coral animal takes calcium from the water to build a hard rock around itself.

It lives inside the rock.

Year after year, millions of the tiny animals die, leaving their coral rocks to pile up.

These make large coral rocks of different colors and shapes.

Eyed coral

Pink coral

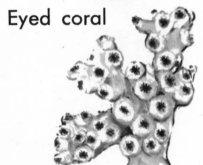

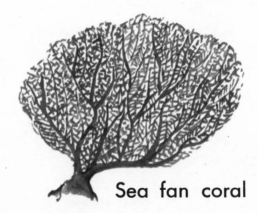

Sea fan coral

See how millions of
tiny pieces of coral
rock have piled up to
form islands in the sea.

The third kind of rock is metamorphic rock. Metamorphic rock is formed when igneous and sedimentary rocks are changed. Sometimes the movements within the earth cause pressure upon igneous or sedimentary rocks.

Here it is very warm. The pressure on top of the rocks is very great. Heat and pressure cause the crystals in the rocks to move. They also cause the crystals to change from one kind to another.

The changes in the crystals make the rocks look different. Now they are metamorphic rocks.

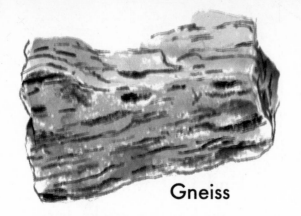

Gneiss

Schist

Some granite rocks
change. Special new
crystals form in bands.
These bands are quite
far apart.

Some granite-like
rocks show many layers
of crystals. These
are close together.

Marble was once
limestone rock.

Quartzite was once
sandstone rock.

REMEMBER

IGNEOUS ROCKS

All igneous rocks come from magma
or from lava.

Magma in the earth cools slowly and
forms igneous rocks with large crystals.
Lava on the earth cools quickly and
forms igneous rocks with small crystals.

SEDIMENTARY ROCKS

Sedimentary rocks are made from
sediments held closely together.

Sediments may be tiny particles of rock,
pebbles, shells and skeletons of animals,
or parts of plants.

METAMORPHIC ROCKS

Metamorphic rocks are made from
igneous and sedimentary rocks pushed
and squeezed deep into the earth.

Heat and pressure cause the crystals to
change and form metamorphic rock.

ROCKS WEAR AWAY

Rocks on the earth are changing size and shape.
When rain washes away soil from around
the rocks on a hill, they will tumble down.
Down roll the rocks.

Falling rocks break
into many pieces.
Large pieces are broken
when they hit each other.

Running water makes rocks wear away.
The water carries sand, mud, and
small rocks from one place to another.

Some rivers empty into the sea. Some
water runs into lakes and ponds.

When the water stops
running, the mud, sand,
and bits of rocks fall to
the bottom and become
sediments.

Rocks change each other.
Rocks hit each other when
they tumble in running water.
See the sharp edges of
rocks before they bump.

The rocks bump many times
as they move along in the
water. The sharp edges
are worn smooth.

The sand moving in brooks rubs over rocks in the bottom. The rocks are scraped by the sand. The rocks grow smaller and smaller.

Many rocks become very smooth.

Rocks at a sandy beach
are worn smooth.

Sometimes when water first sinks into the ground, it becomes an acid.

An acid can eat into limestone. It can eat large holes in limestone rock. These large holes are caves.

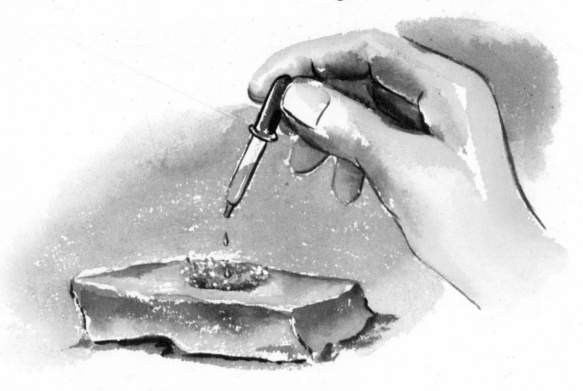

An acid such as vinegar makes limestone fizz. Any rock that fizzes with vinegar is limestone.

A cave like this can be hundreds of feet long.
It takes thousands of years for large caves
to form under the ground.

Ice, too, wears away rock.

When it rains, water fills the tiny holes and cracks in rocks. When winter comes, this water freezes. Ice takes up more room than water. The ice breaks the rocks apart.

This rock is slowly breaking apart.

REMEMBER

Rocks falling down the sides of hills or mountains may break into pieces.

Rocks falling down the sides of hills or mountains may strike each other and break into smaller pieces.

Rocks carried along by running water may strike each other and be broken into smaller pieces.

Running water contains tiny rock particles and pebbles that rub over other rocks and make them smooth.

Acid in the ground eats into rocks made of limestone.

Water freezing in cracks of rocks expands and breaks the rocks into smaller pieces.

LIFE IN THE ROCKS

Sometimes rocks can tell us things about life long ago. Sometimes the remains or prints of plants or animals can be found in rocks. Any such trace of prehistoric plants or animals is called a fossil.

Prehistoric animals made footprints in the mud or sand. When the mud hardened, the print of the foot remained.

Sometimes the whole bodies of animals sank deep into the mud. As the mud dried and hardened into rock, the soft parts of the animals disappeared. But some of the bones or perhaps the whole skeleton was preserved in rock.

Sometimes the air could not reach the buried plants and animals. This kept certain parts of them from rotting away. As the mud or sand hardened to rock, the bones, shells, or leaves buried there turned to rock, too.

This fossil shows several forms of sea life.

Most fossils are found in sedimentary rocks.

This fossil is
the print of a leaf.

This fossil is the
footprint of a dinosaur.

This fossil is the actual
leaves of plants which have
turned to rock.

This fossil is
worm burrows
in rock.

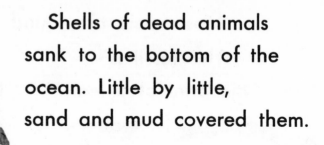

Shells of dead animals
sank to the bottom of the
ocean. Little by little,
sand and mud covered them.

Sometimes shells fell apart
after a long time. Only
the shape of the shell was
left in the sand or mud
which hardened around it.

ROCKS ARE USEFUL

Rocks are used for many different things.

Some rocks are very hard. Granite is a hard igneous rock that is used in making big buildings.

Granite lasts a long time. It does not crumble as soft rocks do.

Granite is good for steps, too.

Hard shale is a sedimentary
rock. This shale is useful
for building roads.

Tiny rocks of hard shale
help to make roads smooth.

Chert

Chert is a sedimentary rock that looks like glass. As chert is broken, it makes sharp edges. It is used for tools, and Indians used it to make arrowheads.

Obsidian, too, is an igneous rock that is used for making tools.

Indians made arrowheads and spearheads from chert and obsidian rock.

Flagstone is a hard sedimentary rock. It is made in layers. When flagstone is split, either by nature or by man, it falls into flat pieces. These flat pieces of rock are used to make pretty walks.

Slate is a hard metamorphic rock. Slate splits into flat pieces also.

Some chalkboards are made from slate rocks.

Some rocks are beautiful.
Marble is a beautiful
metamorphic rock. It is
easy to cut, too. Marble
is used in many ways.

Sometimes man takes the crystals or minerals from the rocks. He uses these in special ways.

Mica is used for the heating parts of electric toasters and irons.

Quartz is used in the lenses of microscopes.

Feldspar is useful in the manufacture of pottery and fine china.

Although man is using rocks and some rocks are wearing away, there will always be rocks.

Right now, sediments are settling in quiet waters. New sedimentary rocks are slowly being made.

Magma, filling new cracks within the earth, is forming new igneous rocks.

And somewhere deep in the earth, old rocks are being pushed down and squeezed. In time, heat and pressure will make them into new metamorphic rocks.

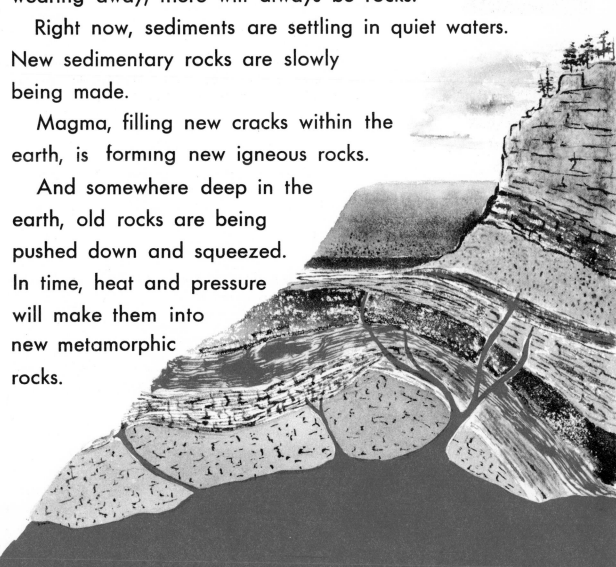

PICTURE DICTIONARY

CRYSTAL A very small piece of nonliving matter. Most crystals have several flat surfaces and pointed corners. 8

FOSSIL Any trace of prehistoric animals or plants found in rocks or hard surfaces on the earth. Fossils can be anything from the whole skeleton of an animal to leaf prints preserved in rocks. 36

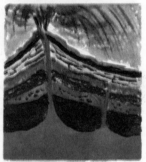

LAVA Hot, liquid rock matter that pours out from under the ground through a volcano. After the liquid matter has cooled and hardened, it is also called lava. 12

MAGMA Hot, liquid rock matter that is beneath the surface of the earth. Igneous rock is formed from magma. 10

SEDIMENTS Rock particles that are carried along by wind, water, or ice and finally deposited at one place or another. Sediments can also be fish shells or coral rocks. 16

VOLCANO A hole in the earth from which hot rock matter and steam pour out. The rock matter forms a hill or mountain as it cools. 12